DESIGN AND TECHNOLOGY

Textiles

BERYL AUSTONI • PENNY LUCAS

SERIES EDITORS: PETER BRANSON • JONATHON RENAUDON-SMITH

CAMBRIDGE UNIVERSITY PRESS

Published by the Press Syndicate of the University of Cambridge
The Pitt Building, Trumpington Street, Cambridge CB2 1RP
40 West 20th Street, New York, NY 10011–4211, USA
10 Stamford Road, Oakleigh, Melbourne 3166, Australia

First published 1996

Printed in Great Britain at the University Press, Cambridge

A catalogue record for this book is available from the British Library

ISBN 0 521 48389 1

Cover – sequined Dr Martens.

Cover design by Ralf Zeigermann

Illustrations by Eikon Design & Illustration, Leicester

Acknowledgements

The authors would like to thank Joyce Lucas and Lucy
Marshall who taught them to sew.

The authors and publisher would like to thank the following
for their help in the preparation of this book.

Yvonne Haggart and all the staff at Aquascutum Ltd.;
Peta Flint and her staff;
Glaxo Wellcome plc;
The Grafton Centre, Cambridge;
Brian Brady, Peter Clarke, Kerry Drage, Elaine Hall, Jamie
Levett, Joanne Logue, Leanne McAlpine, Sandra Mills,
Caroline Perkins and Graham Ward at R. Griggs;
The Manager and staff at Dr Martens, Covent Garden;
Rachel Hargreaves and all the staff at Racing Green;
Brian Dickie and all the staff at Skopos.

The publisher would like to thank the following for
permission to reproduce copyright photographs.

By permission of Northampton Museums and Art Gallery,
19tr, 19tl, 20tr, 20br, 21tr, 21bl, 22tl;
J Sainsbury plc, 6;
Skopos, 40–41, 44–45;
Tony Stone Images/Ed Pritchard, 15tr;
Tony Stone Images/George Kavanagh, 15bl.

Location and studio photography by Graham Portlock:
7, 8, 10–11, 12–13, 23, 24–5, 27, 28, 29, 30, 31, 34, 35, 36,
53b, 54br, 55, 59, 60, 61, 62, 63, 68–9, 70–1, 73, cover;
Andrew Lambert: 42–3, 45, 46–7, 49.

Contents

The product development process

SKOPOS *Design brief*

AQUASCUTUM *Specification and quality indicators*

PETA FLINT *Conceptual design*

SOCKS FOR EVERYONE *Presentation of ideas and evaluation*

AQUASCUTUM/DR MARTENS *Final specification*

PETA FLINT *Design for marketable production*

RACING GREEN *Production plan and schedule*

AQUASCUTUM/DR MARTENS/SKOPOS *Production*

DR MARTENS/RACING GREEN *Launch/Marketing*

Shopping

Shopping has changed, and continues to change and develop, in many ways. For example, the shopping areas in every town have altered from a collection of mainly family-owned shops to rows of branches of multiples or chain stores.

Multiples are large groups owned by national and international companies and are sometimes franchised to individuals. An example of a **franchiser** is Benetton. Local people or groups rent premises and then buy stock from Benetton.

This system means that companies can develop and grow without too much capital outlay or risk for the franchiser.

A High Street in the 1960s.

(Capital outlay is the money needed to buy stock and pay overheads, such as rent for premises, staff pay, costs of heating and lighting, etc.)

One big change in recent years is the development of out-of-town shopping centres, or malls as they are called in the USA where the idea began. These centres were designed to reduce the traffic problems in old town centres, but now they are being criticised for causing the 'death' of town centres. This means that shops close down because people no longer shop there. Government and local authorities are now giving more thought to these problems when considering planning applications.

Out-of-town centres provide easy parking and comfortable shopping in a traffic-free environment. However, the selection of shops is often limited to the multiples who can afford the high rents charged by the developers of these centres. You may have noticed when you have been on holiday abroad that other countries have different styles of shopping.

Survey your local town and area to see how the pattern of shopping has changed in recent years. You might interview an older person you know so that you can get a wider picture of the changes which have taken place in the past.

Inside a shopping centre.

An out-of-town shopping centre.

A typical High Street in 1995.

Shopping by post

For a variety of reasons an increasing number of people are choosing to shop for clothes and household items from mail-order catalogues and newspaper or magazine advertisements. One reason is the increased use of credit and payment cards which makes ordering very easy and quick, particularly if you use the telephone to place orders.

Mail-order shopping has become big business, but who uses this method of shopping? What do they buy and why do they use this method of buying goods rather than, or as well as, going to the shops?

Mail-order catalogues.

Research who buys from mail order, what they buy and why they use this method of shopping. You can do this in a group, in pairs or by yourself.

Find out by surveying people at home, near where you live, at school, etc. You could use a database to record any information, or you could use a chart like the one below.

	What they buy	Why they use mail order
Ralph		
Katie		
Jeshal		
Ikem		

Now that you have discovered who buys what and why, you need to look at the variety of mail-order shopping which is available. With this selection of mail-order catalogues and advertising you can examine the services offered.

Collect examples which illustrate the range of sources of mail-order shopping. Try to find more than one example of each type, for example two large catalogues, so that you can compare prices, illustrations, layout, etc. Make a list of all the types of mail order you have collected.
Examine the catalogues and advertisements to see how clearly they describe and illustrate the goods they are selling. Write a brief report on your findings.

Postage, delivery and returns

When collecting the catalogues and advertisements you will have discovered that the cost of postage and packing, which can add considerably to the cost of the items, is not always included in the price.

A common problem when ordering goods from a catalogue or advertisement is that the item may be out of stock. If you order by post then you may not find out about this for some time as delivery can take up to 28 days. When you order by telephone the salesperson should be able to tell you whether an item is in stock and how long it will take to deliver. If the item required is out of stock, you are usually told the expected date of delivery and can make an informed choice about whether you want to wait for restocking, or try elsewhere. Mail-order companies need to have reliable manufacturers and a good stock control system, so that they can give reliable information to their customers.

The systems for returning goods may also vary and can be costly. Mail-order companies need to have simple systems for returning unwanted goods, without too much cost or inconvenience for the customer. This is very important as the customer cannot see or handle the merchandise before ordering and may be disappointed when it arrives and looks nothing like the picture in the catalogue!

Company	Postage and packing	Delivery times	Total cost	Return procedures etc.

Check all the catalogues and advertisements you have collected for:
• postage and packing costs,
• delivery times,
• return procedures and cost to the customer.

Display your findings in chart form; you could use the computer for this.

Now list the companies with:
• the cheapest and most expensive post and packing,
• the shortest and longest delivery times,
• the simplest and most complicated return procedures.

 ## Guarantees

If things go wrong when you buy items by mail order you have the same rights as when buying items from shops. However, it may be more difficult to complain. If you bought a pair of shoes from a shop and the heel fell off the first time you wore them, you would be able to take them back to the shop and complain. It may not be so simple to return a faulty item you purchased from an advertisement in a news-paper or magazine.

 ## Prices

You may have discovered that prices vary from one catalogue to another for items which seem to be the same or similar. How do these prices compare with those of the shops in the High Street? If the prices are much higher then cus-tomers will not pay for the convenience of shop-ping from home.

Check all your catalogues and advertisements for guarantees. Write a brief report of your findings and make some recommendations about this.

Duvet covers available from a catalogue.

You should now understand:
- **how to plan and conduct research,**
- **how to write a survey or questionnaire,**
- **how to use a database to handle your information,**
- **how to examine the market.**

TASK

You will now be able to complete the task below which may form part of your coursework.

Select *five* items from your catalogues and advertisements and compare the prices with the same or similar items on sale in your local shops. If you or your family have purchased items recently you could use these for the comparison. Design a chart to record your findings. Which is the cheaper, shop or mail order? Write up your conclusions remembering to comment on quality as well as price.

A duvet cover and pillowcase bought in a High Street shop.

Shirts available from a catalogue.

A shirt bought in a High Street shop.

The mail-order company

I t is a complex business to set up and run a mail-order company, whether it is a large or small operation.

A mail-order company needs:
- premises from which to operate – these can be very small, for example the spare bedroom, or a large industrial unit,
- staff to take orders and process them, and to pack and dispatch goods,
- systems to record orders, sales, stock and customers,
- designers to design goods for inclusion in a catalogue and the catalogue itself,
- manufacturers to produce the goods,
- managers to operate the company and ensure that they comply with legal requirements.

Racing Green was founded in 1992 to provide 'comfortable, reasonably priced clothes in good quality fabrics and great colours' according to the Managing Director. Many people use mail order because it is more convenient to order goods at home than to go to the shops.

Operating the company

The business does not have to be on one site. The design team may be based on one site and the warehouse on another. The design team are responsible for the development of the catalogue and the design of the clothes which go into production for each season. The catalogue contains certain staple items, but will also contain new and seasonal designs.

A specification is produced for each of the garments.

The specification will include:
- the fabric to be used,
- the sizes,
- the exact measurements,
- the colours,
- delivery time.

Without a specification, **quality control** would be a problem. Manufacturers need exact instructions for the construction of any items produced for sale in bulk. This will ensure that every garment

Spread from Racing Green catalogue.

is exactly the same measurement and colour and is sewn in the same way. For example a given size must always be cut to fit the same measurements so that a customer can be sure that it will be the correct size. Large companies always have written specifications which are issued to suppliers – incoming goods are then checked against the specification and returned if they are faulty. Suppliers manufacture to a set standard. The fabrics are sometimes purchased in bulk to ensure uniformity on a long run of a garment which is likely to be popular and changes little from one season to another.

Look in a catalogue and identify the garments which are likely to be 'good sellers' for several seasons.
Think about and list what makes a 'good seller' and use a computer design program to design such an item for production in textiles as part of your coursework.

The computer system holds information about customers and stock, and enables the company to run efficiently and supply a quality service to customers. Customer records are held on a database, which could include the name, address, telephone number and information about past purchases. The database is very valuable to the company and could be sold to other companies. The company is bound by the **Data Protection Act** and must operate strictly to its code of conduct. The computer system may also store information about stock levels, pricing and data about items and warehousing. The system must run smoothly because efficient operation of the company relies upon the computer system working well. Customers ordering by telephone will want to know whether an item is in stock and the expected delivery time when they order; the computer system enables the salesperson to advise them about this accurately.

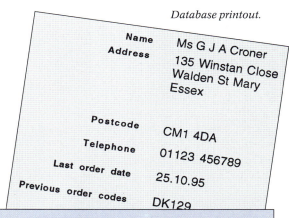

Database printout.

Name	Ms G J A Croner
Address	135 Winstan Close Walden St Mary Essex
Postcode	CM1 4DA
Telephone	01123 456789
Last order date	25.10.95
Previous order codes	DK129

Use a database on a computer in school or at home. Design a database for use in your work for Textiles. This could hold information about fibres or fabrics, sets of measurements for products, or useful addresses for supplies or research.

Once you can use a database, you will find it useful for project work.

Find out about the Data Protection Act, what it does and how it can be of use to you and your family.

All shirts are 100% cotton, machine washable and come in sizes 8, 10, 12, 14, 16.

Processing an order

Orders come in to the company by both post and telephone. Orders received by post are sorted, checked and put into batches. They have an order number attached to them which helps with identification if there are problems. Orders are checked by hand as well as by the computer.

Telephone orders are answered in strict rotation – the call will go to any salesperson who is free at the time. Calls always need a prompt response, otherwise a sale may be lost if a customer gets tired of waiting for the call to be answered. This is especially important at busy times such as when a new catalogue has been launched. The length of a call is also important. Since a customer is paying for the call they need to be dealt with as quickly as possible without making them feel rushed into a decision. All the ordering and processing is completed by the salesperson using the computer terminal and the information is passed directly to the warehouse.

The warehouse operation

Goods come into the warehouse from suppliers and a sample will be checked by the quality control team to ensure that it meets the specification set by the designers. Once this has been completed the goods are stored in their allotted place in the warehouse. Each item has a location which is recorded on the computer.

A completed order form.

Call centre.

When an order is placed, the computer system will sort the items into order so that the operator can walk around the warehouse and 'pick' the items easily without walking further than necessary. All warehouses are now designed in this way which makes the operation of selecting items for individual orders much quicker and simpler for the people involved.

Presentation is important to mail-order companies. Goods are packed very carefully using boxes and tissue paper. This is a lengthy process, but it is worthwhile as the goods look attractive and arrive undamaged. Parcels are despatched by post. There may be a bar code on the parcel which is scanned and recorded on the computer system so that in the event of a problem there is proof of despatch.

A clothing warehouse.

Look at the packaging of goods bought in shops and through mail order and write a report on your findings, focusing on the different needs for the packaging of goods.

What makes good packaging for garments?

Bar code reading.

The history of shoes

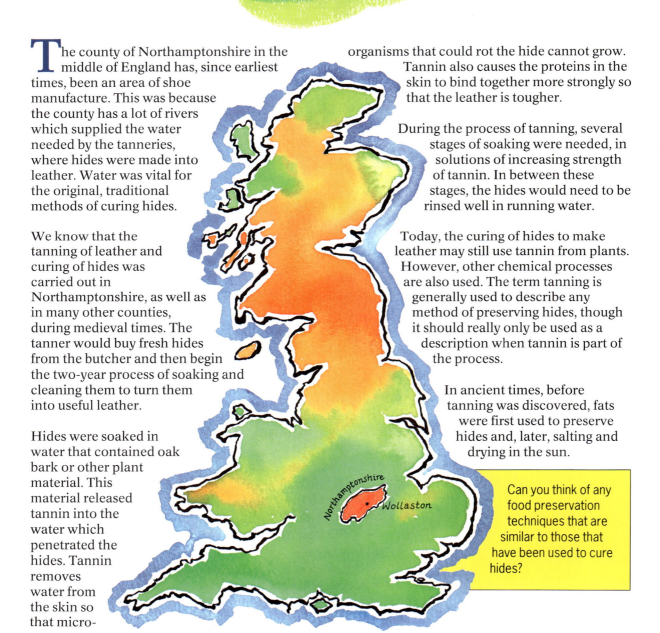

The county of Northamptonshire in the middle of England has, since earliest times, been an area of shoe manufacture. This was because the county has a lot of rivers which supplied the water needed by the tanneries, where hides were made into leather. Water was vital for the original, traditional methods of curing hides.

We know that the tanning of leather and curing of hides was carried out in Northamptonshire, as well as in many other counties, during medieval times. The tanner would buy fresh hides from the butcher and then begin the two-year process of soaking and cleaning them to turn them into useful leather.

Hides were soaked in water that contained oak bark or other plant material. This material released tannin into the water which penetrated the hides. Tannin removes water from the skin so that micro-organisms that could rot the hide cannot grow. Tannin also causes the proteins in the skin to bind together more strongly so that the leather is tougher.

During the process of tanning, several stages of soaking were needed, in solutions of increasing strength of tannin. In between these stages, the hides would need to be rinsed well in running water.

Today, the curing of hides to make leather may still use tannin from plants. However, other chemical processes are also used. The term tanning is generally used to describe any method of preserving hides, though it should really only be used as a description when tannin is part of the process.

In ancient times, before tanning was discovered, fats were first used to preserve hides and, later, salting and drying in the sun.

Northamptonshire

Wollaston

Can you think of any food preservation techniques that are similar to those that have been used to cure hides?

Shoe styles

Our knowledge of the footwear of early times is based on pictorial evidence and statuary, on the shoes themselves and on secondary sources such as a record that, in 1266, King Henry III ordered 150 pairs of shoes from Northampton. (They cost four or five pence a pair.)

A Roman Sandal.

Since then advances in materials and production methods have changed the appearance of shoes. People who made the shoes built on their existing skills and creativity by experimenting with new techniques. So, the Roman sandal looks very different from the medieval shoe, which looks very different from modern shoes. The Romans were used to a warm climate and hence wore sandals, even when they invaded colder climes like Great Britain. The sandals were of leather with large-headed nails hammered into the soles. These hobnails protected the leather when walking on the stone-surfaced roads that the Romans built.

Sole of an Egyptian sandal.

Through evidence we have found from the Neolithic and Bronze Age times, we know that humans wrapped animal hide round their feet to create footwear. We also know from wall paintings and grave goods in the pyramids that the early Egyptians wore leather sandals which comprised a sole and toe thong. Ancient Greek statues show a similar style, but with more straps. The styles worn by the Romans were similar to the Greek, but more sturdy. These were worn by people throughout the Roman Empire, even by soldiers on Hadrian's Wall and in Scotland. Britons and Celts of the time also wore thonged footwear, despite the wet weather conditions.

After the Romans left England other invaders brought a different lifestyle and culture. The Roman roads were not maintained and the hobnail also fell into disuse. The turnshoe, where the upper and sole were seamed together inside out and then turned, became the predominant style of shoe.

After the Norman conquest of England stronger materials produced from tougher hides made by improved tanning methods were used to make shoes. The shoes were more hardwearing, but the style was still turnshoe.

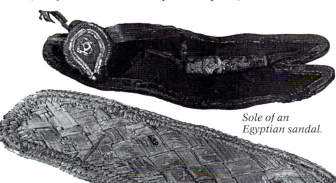
Medieval shoe.

At the end of the Middle Ages the method for constructing shoes changed to a welted shoe. This is where the upper is first attached to the insole and welt, then a second row of stitching attaches the welt (see page 29) to the sole. The hollow made by the addition of the welt was filled with a cork mixture. The other change in construction was to move the main upper seam to the centre back, producing the shape of shoe with which we are familiar today.

Fashion has also played its part, but only for people who could afford to be fashionable.

Of the shoes that have survived from earlier centuries to the modern day the majority are those that would have belonged to ladies of the wealthier classes.

> Carry out research on shoes that have survived from earlier centuries. Would they have belonged to wealthy or poor people, men or women? Why do you think these shoes have survived whilst others have not? (Think about cost, use and storage.)

Boots and shoes have, at one time or another, been made from almost every material imaginable. As advances in technology have offered new materials, many of these have been adapted for shoe use. The development of synthetic materials, and combinations of materials such as fabric and resin, or leather and foam, and the development of increasingly more sophisticated machinery to work these materials, has extended the range of choice for the manufacturer. Despite these developments leather has always remained the preferred material for making shoes.

> What materials are used now as well as leather?

In Britain, before medieval times, people would have made their own shoes. Later, as skills and techniques developed, there was often a village bootmaker, who would still have made the

Eighteenth-century shoes.

Liberty shoes from 1940s with box.

whole shoe, but for other people as well as his own family. Prior to the 1850s all aspects of boot and shoe manufacture were completed by hand. Even when **labour was divided**, during the Industrial Revolution, and **outworkers** performed separate tasks such as stitching and seaming, all of which contributed eventually to the whole shoe, the work was still done by hand.

Mechanisation came later to the shoe trade than in other industries, such as weaving, during the **Industrial Revolution**. With mechanisation came the development of factories where the work was done. This was because the new machinery was heavy and expensive, and unsuitable for use in the home. With the introduction of machinery such as the Blake sole sewing machine (1864) and the Goodyear welting machine (1872) it was no longer feasible for these processes to be done at home.

Closing, the stitching together of the parts of the shoe, was still carried out by homeworkers. This could involve up to 30 different processes, including stamping of the size, fancy stitching and seaming. Sometimes the sewing machines used were rented by the homeworker from the manufacturer.

'Cloud and Rainbow' shoe, 1979.

Union Jack shoe, 1953. Balmoral boot, c. 1920.

The increased levels of production, which came as a result of the greater mechanisation of the processes in factories, meant that more goods were available at a cheaper cost. So more people could afford to buy more shoes. This made it possible for 'fashion' to become more significant in the design of footwear as people could afford to choose for style rather than just for the function of the footwear.

Despite the advances there still remained a demand for high-quality, hand-made footwear. Highly skilled craftsmen continued to produce hand-made shoes as they do today.

You should now:
- **understand how to research,**
- **have a knowledge of the materials used in shoe making.**

You will now be able to complete the task below which may form part or all of your coursework.

Working as a group collect information about shoe styles through the centuries. You will find books a valuable resource, but paintings and statues can also provide evidence. You will probably find more information about recent decades. Make a display of your findings and prepare a presentation to describe the main developments in shoe styles. Can you identify any recurring fashion themes? Describe and comment on them.

The history of Dr Martens

R. Griggs, who are the makers of Dr Martens, have been boot and shoe manufacturers for more than 90 years. They are still based in Wollaston in Northamptonshire, UK.

Military boot.

Benjamin Griggs and Septimus Jones opened their village bootmaking partnership in 1901. That partnership split up in 1910 at which time Benjamin's son Reginald joined his father to form R. Griggs and Co. The components for the boots were made by outworkers who lived in the local cottages. The components were then taken to the firm's factory to be screwed and stitched to make military and agricultural boots. These were called 'Bulldog' boots and manufacture of these boots continued, using the same production methods, until the mid 1940s.

The history of R. Griggs tells us something of history generally. Find out:
- why 'cottage industries' have that name,
- why there would have been a particular demand for military and agricultural boots up until 1945,
- why they might have chosen the name 'Bulldog' to describe the boots.

By the 1950s, when the third generation of the Griggs family were managing the company, it had not grown in size. There was, however, strong competition from 'Tuf' working boots.

These had vulcanised rubber soles, produced by a chemical treatment of rubber which makes it hardwearing. This production method allowed for much higher output than Griggs' traditional methods because the vulcanising was a completely mechanical process and so less labour intensive than making shoes by hand.

Find out from someone who would have bought shoes in the 1960s whether or not they remember 'Tuf' shoes. They were made for adults and children, boys and girls. Ask them to describe what they remember about the shoes and for what purpose they were bought. Share your findings with others in your working group.

Griggs met this challenge by uniting with the other shoe manufacturers in Wollaston to form a **co-operative** to produce their own vulcanised soles. However, despite their success, they were simply meeting an existing challenge, and not developing and making innovations.

Their greatest development was to come from an unexpected source – a medical man who lived in Germany. Dr Claus Maertens had injured his foot in a skiing accident.

Dr. AirWair Martens

WITH Bouncing SOLES

'Air Wair' logo.

To ease the pain of walking he made himself a special pair of shoes, the soles of which he constructed from old tyres. These soles had air trapped within closed compartments, and provided cushioning for the foot. This was necessary because the action of walking jars the ankle.

Working with an old student friend, Herbert Funck, Claus patented and marketed the 'Dr Maertens' shoes, which became extremely popular in Germany. The product had great potential for selling in a world market.

name was anglicised). The first UK pair was made on 1 April 1960 (hence the name '1460s'). Various companies within the Wollaston co-operative used their own brand names, perhaps the best known is R. Griggs' own 'Air Wair'.

In the late 1960s 'DMs' became the essential item of clothing for young people: a pair of 'Doc Martens cherry reds' were the vital fashion item. They were also extremely comfortable and had a wider market; to anyone who spends a lot of time on their feet DMs are not a fashion item, but a practicality.

Dr Martens are durable, comfortable and perceived by many to be stylish. Today they are bought by all types of people, including rock stars, nurses, bankers and the police.

Originally the Dr Martens boots were available from ordinary retail shoe shops and were the only element in the 'Doc Martens culture'. Because of their popularity and evident widespread appeal Dr Martens have been expanded into the broader fashion field. They are now produced in a wide range of styles and materials.

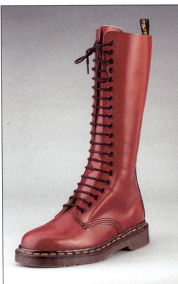

Dr Martens Cherry Reds.

Cross section of Dr Martens.

Sandwich several layers of bubble plastic between two sheets of thin card. Make another sandwich with newspaper between the card. The two 'sandwiches' should look the same, and be labelled A and B.

Research, by asking friends and testing for yourself, which are the most comfortable to stand on, barefoot, for a period of time. Do you now understand the principle of the Dr Martens sole? Explain.

It was because of the success of Wollaston vulcanising that R. Griggs and the Wollaston companies were offered the UK rights to make the boots which were called Dr Martens (the

The Dr Martens philosophy has developed since the boots were first designed but still retains a commitment to the original workwear products. The styles they now have reflect this commitment within a broader fashion context, that is styles developed from workwear that also cater for individuality and a market which is less conventional.

The Covent Garden store.

In late 1994, the first Dr Martens department store was opened in Covent Garden, London. The shop has five storeys and the interior decoration was designed to reflect the Dr Martens style, including lots of exposed brickwork, iron, concrete and steel, and yellow stitching all over the place! The building looks like a factory, or industrial unit. It is an appropriate place for selling boots whose predecessors were plain workwear but are now often seen as sophisticated and even elegant. The price tickets are in metal wire frames; the seating has enlarged shoe vamps, welts and tongues **appliquéd** on to the leather covering; the fitting rooms are enormous hides hung on a metal rail with metal rings. The Dr Martens

Interior of shop.

theme is consistent throughout. Even the leather polish, dubbin and laces are displayed in a way that reflects the overall design style.

The department store sells much more than the boots. You can buy a burger, a DM watch, DM stationery and even get a DM haircut. There is also fashion wear clothing, including children's clothes which are small versions of the adult's clothes, as are the children's shoes. The display of Dr Martens boots, even when you know that there are 150 styles in 3000 permutations, is an eyeopener, and includes materials such as

leopard skin print, tartan, denim, and many others. The shop is great fun to be in, for all age groups, whether they are customers or not.

In the years since Dr Martens were first made, more than 60 million pairs have been made in the United Kingdom. Sales are not confined to the UK and they are exported around the world. Dr Martens, the comfort shoe, have become synonymous with youth and fashion culture the world over.

You should now understand:
- **products and their applications (shoes for specific uses),**
- **materials (leather),**
- **product development (style and use of a variety of materials),**
- **marketing a product.**

You will now be able to complete the tasks below which may form part or all of your coursework.

- Research attitudes to Dr Martens in different age groups. Do a survey of young people who wear DMs and those people who use Dr Martens as workwear. You will need to find out about the reasons for choice, numbers of pairs owned (at any one time or over the years), level of satisfaction and how they feel about other people who wear DMs (i.e. fashion versus work footwear). Write up your findings as a report.
- Identify the workwear requirements (garments and footwear) for several local or national employers (for example, the Post Office).
- Using your IT skills produce a chart which shows the requirements of the employers investigated by the whole group. You should be able to identify requirements common to all.
- Using this information design a basic uniform which meets the requirements of at least two or three employers. Indicate additions/ adaptations which would make the clothing job-specific.
- Make up a prototype of one garment.

Dr Martens – design and pattern technology

Dr Martens 1460s became a design statement in themselves for those who adopted them as an essential part of their 'style'. There have been, and still are, seemingly endless permutations of finish for the basic Dr Martens boot. The variations are predominately in the fabric used for the upper part of the boot because the Air Wair sole remains the same. Traditionally dark, sober black and brown leathers were used. Now there are also bright colours, patent leathers, textiles (ranging from velvet to denim) and even lace on a gold or silver metallic finish leather.

The outstanding success of Dr Martens has meant that the style range has been increased beyond relatively simple adaptations of material. For these developments the company employs a freelance designer.

Any designer needs to know a great deal about the field in which they are working. Designing is a very practical activity, involving much more than the creative process; it is much more than drawing and draughtsmanship. The designer needs to know about the end use for the designed object – this will form a part of the design brief. What is not in the design brief is the background knowledge of the nature of materials in which the design is to be implemented. Even if the materials are to be used in an unusual way which goes above and beyond the accepted boundaries of usage, the designer must be fully informed about them.

The freelance designer employed to design Dr Martens is a specialist shoe designer. It is vital for shoe designers to know not only about the materials in which they are working, but also about the foot itself – how it varies in shape, movement, health; all the things that make feet so useful to human beings. The Dr Martens' designer works to a theme and produces a detailed drawing of the design. This is the first part of the creative process; then begins the task of translating the drawing into a 3-dimensional shoe.

Detailed drawing of design.

DM boots and shoes.

Making the pattern

In the same way that patterns are used to make fabric garments, patterns are also used to make shoes. The principle is exactly the same in the method employed at Aquascutum (see page 56).

A cutter, working with constant reference to the design drawing, creates a pattern from which a sample shoe will be made up. This first pattern is made by hand using simple tools: a knife and card.

Pattern cutter at work.

What is not simple is the fund of knowledge and skill possessed by the pattern cutter, who is interpreting the 2-dimensional drawing to make a 3-dimensional product. At this stage the quality of work is dependent on the competence and experience of the worker.

> Examine one of your own shoes. Using only paper, make a pattern that represents the elements of your shoe. You will notice that there are allowances made for the pieces to be joined. Which of the parts of your shoe are purely functional and which are decorative features? Sketch or photograph your shoe and make a double page display with your pattern.

When the sample shoe has been finished and any necessary adjustment made to the pattern and/or design, it is almost time for the bulk manufacturing process to begin. However, for this the cutters (or 'clickers') in the factory need

a range of pattern sizes from which to cut. The pattern cutter of the past would have had to provide the different size patterns for the 'clickers'. The gradations in pattern size are regular; 8 mm in length and 4.34 mm in width. Before metrication the length difference would have been called $\frac{1}{3}$rd of an inch, a measurement that is still referred to in colloquial conversation.

The process for making a range of sizes of the sample pattern has not changed in years. A simple enlarging device called a **pantograph** would have been used for enlarging. Despite this use of mechanical aid, great care had to be taken. Each new size was made from the one preceding it (so a 5 would be from a 4, and a 6 from a 5). One tiny error would result in all the following patterns being wrong, the error getting larger on each pattern. One way to make a check was to 'knock up' the patterns. That is, the same piece for sizes 3–7, for example the back strip, were held up together with the smallest at the front. The patterns were tapped on a surface so the difference between each of the patterns could be seen and judged to be correct or not.

> Try out the grading up process. Draw a rectangle of width 30 mm and length 80 mm (this is to represent a simple shoe component). This rectangle is size 4. Grade it for all sizes 3 to 7. (Remember that gradation in length between sizes is 8 mm. For the purposes of this exercise, use a gradation in width between sizes of 4 mm.) Check your accuracy by 'knocking up'. How long did the exercise take?

Pattern technologist at work.

> The gradation you have done manually could be more accurately done using a computer graphics program such as Autosketch. Draw your basic shoe/boot pattern using a computer drawing package. Most drawing packages will have a 'scale' command. Start with one size as the 'basic' size and work out what the scaling up and/or down has to be to achieve the next size shoe/boot in the sequence. Use this scale amount to draw your designs on the screen. Print or plot out the shapes and make them up into a shoe/boot shape.

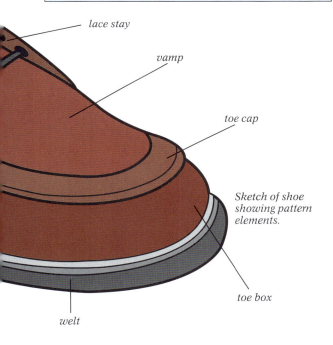

lace stay

vamp

toe cap

Sketch of shoe showing pattern elements.

toe box

welt

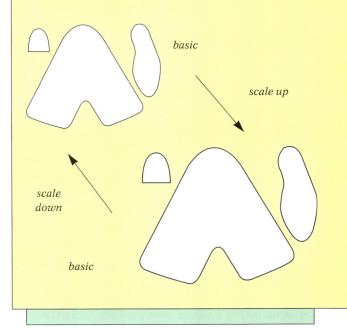

basic

scale up

scale down

basic

Today the sample pattern is passed to a pattern technologist who works with a sophisticated computer program to draft, scale up and cut the patterns. The person working with the computer aided process must have a sound knowledge of shoe construction and would benefit from also being a skilled pattern cutter.

The first task is to transfer the pattern on to the screen. This is done by digitising the pattern pieces, that is changing reference points on the pattern to numbered co-ordinates (rather like a map) which the computer can work from. The standard (side view of the shoe) is put on the screen first and the construction lines of other pieces, such as the quarter, vamp, tongue etc., are added to that. The computer can draw lines

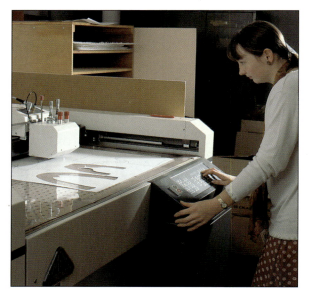

Pattern cutting machine.

in different colours to define different patterns. These colours can be reproduced on the computer printout.

Once the basic pattern has been input to the computer, the full size range can be computed and output very quickly. Before computers were used for the process, it would take an extremely skilled pattern cutter a whole day to complete the range by hand.

The computer is linked to the machine that cuts the patterns from card. It looks rather like a smaller version of the Gerber cutter used at Aquascutum (see page 58). There is a perforated bed through which suction is applied to hold the card in place. The shapes are cut at the computer's instruction, printed with the details of different patterns and even marked with the

lines for stitching detail. The card patterns are then ready to go to the knife maker who makes a 'knife' for the shape of each piece. The making of the boot or shoe can now begin.

At R. Griggs, the whole process of the manufacture of footwear is a fascinating mixture of the most modern technology with the most traditional craft skills. The combination of age-old materials like leather with the modern vulcanised sole, and the alliance of a seemingly delicate lace with the 'don't mess with me' style of the traditional DM boot is unusual.

You should now understand:
- **IT applications,**
- **the recognition of a need for design,**
- **product planning,**
- **use of materials for footwear.**

You will now be able to complete the task below which may form part or all of your coursework.

Taking a basic DM boot as your starting point, provide detailed working instructions for customising the boot. Your developments should be within your own set design brief and should indicate the individual for whom the boot is intended. For example, the boot for a marathon runner might include wings on the heels or an ornithologist might favour feathered boots. Your creativity could include surface decoration of the boot and/or surface additions. It must be safe to wear: a fantasy which could be realised.

Making Dr Martens

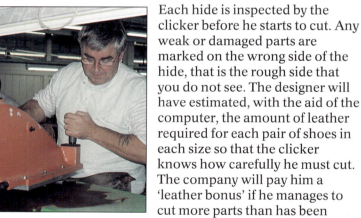

In a small town close to Wollaston there is one of the many factories which make up the company of R. Griggs. When the company was formed it would have been simple to centralise the production onto one large site, but the nature of the shoe industry in the area was such that in each small town there were small factories like this which provided employment for the residents. Griggs chose to continue to operate these small units. This has the advantage that, as certain jobs are mainly done by women who also have families to look after, it is easier for them to work hours that allow them to combine their dual roles, by reducing the time taken to travel to their place of work. This method of production seems rather dated in a time when many companies are using larger, more automated factories, but in this way R. Griggs provides work in smaller centres where it is required and where it helps to preserve those communities by providing income.

Different stages in the process of making footwear are done in different factories, and the finished materials from one factory are moved to the factory where the next stage of processing takes place.

 ## Cutting

The cutting of the leather for the shoe uppers is still called 'clicking' in the industry and the men who do this job (and in 1995 they *were* still all men) are called 'clickers'. The name comes

from the sound that the knife used to make against the frame put around the area to be cut in the days when the cutting was done with a knife. Clicking is a very skilled job as leather is a natural and expensive material and must be used carefully to minimise waste.

Hides are bought in bulk by the company from various countries. In the past the leather was produced locally and tanned in local tanneries, but there are now only a few working tanneries in Northamptonshire.

Cutting.

Each hide is inspected by the clicker before he starts to cut. Any weak or damaged parts are marked on the wrong side of the hide, that is the rough side that you do not see. The designer will have estimated, with the aid of the computer, the amount of leather required for each pair of shoes in each size so that the clicker knows how carefully he must cut. The company will pay him a 'leather bonus' if he manages to cut more parts than has been estimated from a hide. (The shoe industry still operates on a **piece work** system, where the worker is paid for each piece of work they do, and so the cutter must work quickly and accurately if he is to earn more than the standard wage as well as the leather bonus.)

The cutting begins after inspecting and marking the hide. It is done with metal shapes which have been made for the various parts of the shoe and look like odd-shaped biscuit cutters. They are placed on the hide and then pressed down

Trace the three different shoe parts on this page. See how many of each you can cut from a sheet of A4 paper.

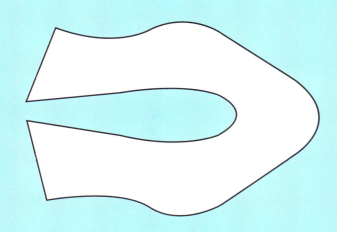

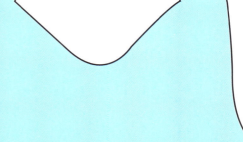

with a press to cut. Unlike cutting out biscuits, you do not start on the edge and work into the centre. This is because the hide is not of equal thickness all over and stretches more across than down, so different pieces need to be cut from different parts of the hide. The top of the shoe is always cut from the centre area of the hide as this part stretches least and so will not go out of shape when the shoe is worn, particularly in wet weather. The small parts, like the tongue which goes under the laces, are cut from the sides of the hide which are usually thinner and are sometimes marked. The leather is the highest cost in the manufacture of the shoe and so must be used carefully. Sometimes a hide is very uneven and pieces must be 'split' to ensure that the leather is of the same thickness on each shoe of a pair. A machine shaves the excess leather from the underside of the pieces after cutting; this is known as skiving. After cutting, the parts are bundled keeping the same size pieces together. (The 'clicker' may sometimes cut parts for two sizes of shoes from the same hides to maximise the use of the leather, so he must take care when bundling the pieces together.) Each bundle is marked with a coloured crayon so that each size can be correctly identified during the making to ensure that the shoes are correctly sized at the end.

At this stage each piece is checked for quality. If a poor quality component is identified at this stage rather than later, the finished shoe will not fail a quality check when it has become part of a potentially expensive pair of shoes.

Diagram of a hide showing the stretch and the thicker areas.

leg

leg

belly – thin area

middle of back – thick area

belly – thin area

leg

leg

Quality checking.

 *Closing*

Once the shapes which form the upper have been cut and checked they move on to the closing room. Here the parts are stitched together to make the top of the shoe. This work is done mainly by women and is very skilled, just like that of machinists in a clothes factory. Some of the machines look like the ones used for clothes but others, called post machines, do not. These have a post rather than a flat bed for sewing on, and are like a free arm domestic sewing machine with the arm rounded and stood on its end.

needed. A further machine may be threaded up with a different coloured or thicker thread to do fancy or top stitching.

> Look at *three* different pairs of shoes and decide how many different machines would have been used to form the production line for the closing stage of production.

Linings and insoles are cut in another of the small factories belonging to the R. Griggs company. These are cut from huge sheets of fabric using an automatic cutter which cuts

Post machine in use.

Closing is a complex procedure and the components move back and forth down the production line in the same way as in a clothes factory, with certain processes being done by each worker according to their skills and the machine they are using. One person may join the side to the back on a flat bed machine, while the next worker in the line will join the side to the front using a post machine to get round the curved shape. If you look at your shoes you will understand why these two types of machine are

several pairs at once. The linings and insoles are also stamped with information about size and shape. In the same factory the insoles are prepared ready for assembly by having a rim stitched around the edge.

Lasting and making

The components which have been made in the various small factories around Wollaston are delivered to the main assembly factory in Wollaston for the shoe to be completed. A **last** is used to form the shape of each pair of shoes. It is made from plastic now, but was originally made from wood.

A last.

When shoes are made entirely by hand for individual customers, the shoemaker will have a last which has been specially made to fit the customer and is adjusted if their feet change shape. There are still a very few shoemakers who make by hand, and shoes made this way usually cost hundreds of pounds a pair.

In the R. Griggs factory, the uppers are placed over the lasts which are arranged in pairs in boxes on a track to move them along the assembly line. The insoles have been temporarily attached to the last with staples so that they do not move during the assembly process. Each pair of shoes has a ticket of work attached and the laced part of the shoe is tied together as it will be when the shoes are worn. In the first stage of the process the toe of the shoe is moulded or lasted over the shape of the last. To do this the leather is steamed to make it

soft and pliable and is stretched over the toe and stapled in place to the rim of the insole. The sides are then lasted in the same way and the surplus leather is trimmed.

At the next stage the welt is sewn to the upper. The welt is the leather or plastic rim around the edge of the upper which will be used to sew the upper to the sole.

Not all shoes have a visible welt and some shoes are made in different ways so that they do not need one.

Sewing the welt to the upper.

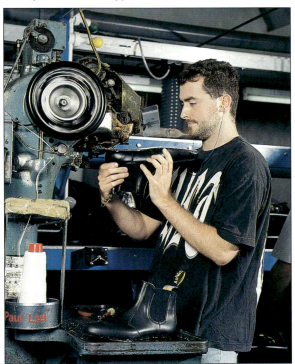

Look at a selection of shoes to see if they have a visible welt. What do you conclude from your observations?

Trimming the edges.

Filling.

Boxing.

The surplus seam is trimmed away just as you would when working with fabric. The shoe is then turned upside down to be bottom filled. The filling that is used is made from a material like carpet and fits between the insole and the sole to cushion the foot. At this stage a wooden shank is placed down the centre of the shoe to support the arch of the foot and the insole of the shoe. It is made from ash wood as this bends easily. Some very high heeled shoes have these made from metal to give extra support.

The sole is now spot welded to the shoe upper to hold it in place whilst it is sealed together. This is done by heating the sole to melt it a little so that it will fuse to the upper. Dr Martens are the only shoes of this type which are welded like this – most others are glued or stitched. The shoe is now complete and the edges are trimmed.

The last is removed (this is called last slipping) and the seat sock, which is a shaped insole-type piece, is put into the heel. Each pair of

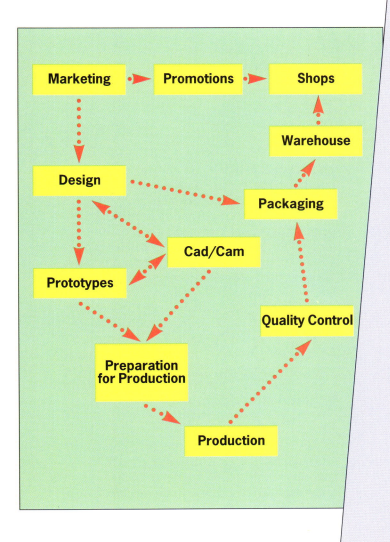

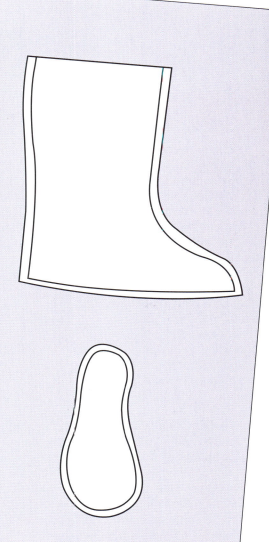

Dr Martens is then cleaned and treated, laced and ticketed and goes to be examined finally for quality. Every pair is examined before it is boxed and sent to the warehouse for distribution.

You should now understand:
• **product planning,**
• **industrial processes and applications,**
• **quality control and assurance.**

You will now be able to complete the task below which may form part or all of your coursework.

- A children's nightwear manufacturer has asked you to design an item of footwear for a child which could be worn with their new range for next season.
- Make up a prototype and cost the footwear.
- Draw up a plan for the production to include details of the production line. This plan could include the stages of production, costings, human resources and timings.

TASK

Skopos

Skopos is a design-based textile company who sell their own fabrics, wallcoverings, accessories and furniture. They offer, however, much more than the goods themselves. The fabrics can be made up at their own workshops into upholstery, curtains, bedspreads and all types of soft furnishings. They also offer a complete Interior Design Consultancy Service.

Skopos could comprise a world of interior design almost entirely by itself, because they design/manufacture most things required for interior design.

skopos

FABRICS & WALLCOVERINGS

The company was founded in 1971 by three students who had just completed their studies at Batley School of Art, in Yorkshire which is the traditional home of woollen mills. They started the company with limited resources but were fortunate to be looking for premises in an area where the large spaces offered by the old textile mills were no longer in demand. They found part of an old woollen mill to rent in Dewsbury. The building was, and still is, called Providence Mills.

Providence Mills.

The early years of the company were a struggle but the products were their own excellent advertisement and the business grew. They had started printing on a 20-metre long hand printing table, but then progressed to 50-metre long tables. This not only increased their volume of production, but also meant that the designs could progress from one and two colours to four and five colours. Although the length of table has no effect on the possible number of colours for printing, a short table is not practical for more than two colour printing because there is a more frequent need for changing the printing screens.

At this stage the target market for Skopos, although remaining **wholesale**, grew from schools (their original main purchaser) to hotels and hospitals. Goods were still produced on a **contract basis** to the specifications of individual customers. The market was further opened up when they bought the whole of the Dewsbury Mill and decided to advance to automatic printing. This allowed them to expand the colour range to between 10 and 15 for one design.

Find out why places like the woollen mill in Dewsbury were no longer needed for the production of woollen fabrics. You might find it useful to research historical and geographical sources.

This step forward meant that the Skopos textiles were now in demand for the home market as well as the contract market because the designs appealed to a wider market in more colours. The company was thus launched into the **retail** trade.

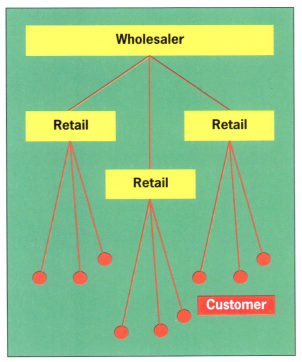

The difference between wholesale and retail.

Either draw/trace the picture on the right or generate your own line drawing using your IT skills. You need three copies of the picture. Working in teams of three, use coloured pencils, crayons, paints, collage or any other appropriate medium to put colour on each of the pictures. On one use only two colours, on the second use five colours and on the third use 10 to 15 colours. (You can, on all of the pictures, leave some areas uncoloured to represent the background fabric.)The visual impact of your three coloured pictures will vary greatly. With others in your team decide which number of colours you prefer and why. Make note of how you think the number of colours in the design could affect its use for soft furnishings.

The product range at Skopos developed as printing techniques became more sophisticated and the market for the home grew.

With such a large product range available the shops owned by the company became **module retailers**. They were able to supply, from stock or order, the full Skopos range and thereby meet the customer need for an entire service.

Visual representation of module retailer.

Although Skopos products today, with their richness of style and colour are a far cry from the bold and simple designs of 1971, they are still part of the same design concept. This is because they result from the same ethos held by those three Batley students. The original Skopos ethos was to produce effective and eyecatching designs which were cheap to produce and would fill a gap in the market. The goal now is still to fill a gap in the market, though this is a very different gap, with the increased sophistication of the products and their style. What has remained constant is the fact that the company's work is design-led.

SKOPOS PRODUCT RANGE				
Flame retardant fabrics	Wallcoverings	Upholstery	Soft furnishings	Accessories
printed 100% cotton	fabric backed and	sofas	curtains	cushions
sateens	vinyl wallpapers and	chairs	pelmets	bean bags
jacquard weaves	borders	sofa beds	tiebacks	floor cushions
sheers	lining papers	occasional chairs	blinds	trimmings
voiles	adhesives	footstools	quilted bedspreads	tracks
plains			duvet covers	poles
quilted pieces			headboards	curtain accessories
linings			feather duvets	
printed blackouts			pillows	

Compile a project which will show your understanding of the range of Skopos products. Your pictures and samples will not necessarily be of Skopos products, but of similar products from other manufacturers. They will show what is available in the wider market place. To do this collect pictures, take photographs, make your own drawings and write descriptions of, for example, soft furnishings, wall-coverings and other items included in the Skopos range. Look at the activity on page 47 and link your choice of pictures to the settings described there.

Fabric design and testing

When we see new clothes, cars, furniture – in fact any new product – it is very easy to take what we see at face value: that is to be aware simply of the visual image, and forget about the work that has gone into achieving that image. It is important to remember that what we see is the result of a long and carefully managed design process.

This is certainly true of Skopos products whatever the market, contract, wholesale or retail.

In 1971, with their basic equipment, the company were producing simple geometric designs, often in single colourways (using only one colour). With increased technical innovation in both production and designing the designs have become more sophisticated. The design process itself may have become more complex as the company has grown, but it

A simple geometric design.

was very definitely in place in the early days. Simple styles often require as much design effort as more complex ones.

The company has a design studio where new collections are developed. The designers work to a set design brief. This could include, for example, incorporating a house logo into the design for a company fabric, developing existing patterns, identifying gaps within the range or working on suggestions from clients.

The designers have to work within the constraints of the technical capabilities of their equipment and the materials they use. These would be such things as numbers of colours used and width of fabric. Once the brief has been set the designer begins the research. As in any research, information can be found almost anywhere, sometimes in the most unlikely places. When you are involved in any research activity you would be wise always to be alert for information that might be of use to you. For instance, if you were undertaking research for children's wallpaper designs, you might find ideas from a collection of children's birthday cards for your designs.

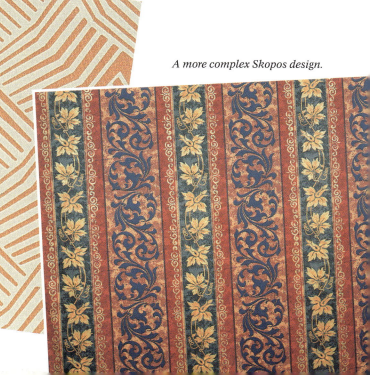

A more complex Skopos design.

Brief

↓

Investigation

↓

Ideas

↓

Evaluation

↓

Development

↓

Planning

↓

Realisation

↓

Testing

↓

Evaluation

Design process.

The theme board serves as a direct information source when the designer begins the work of drawing out the pattern. In the Skopos Design Studio development sheets, the designer's working drawings, are reviewed by the Design Team once every two weeks. Once the artwork has been approved sample printing screens are used to develop the different colourways.

Skopos produces up to four collections a year. Each will include four or five feature design fabrics (used for curtains and upholstery) and four or five complementary fabrics. The complementary fabrics reflect the feature designs but are less striking and serve to enhance the main fabrics. They would be used for cushions and other accessories. Each of the fabrics will be manufactured in each of the colourways.

Example of development sheet.

The designer will set up a theme board on which the research is displayed. Information could take the form of pictures, notes and drawings. If, for example, the theme for the new fabric was Elizabethan, the board might include photographs of Tudor buildings, the designer's own drawing of architectural details, a postcard of a painting of Queen Elizabeth I, an enlargement of a Tudor Rose and some notes about heraldic devices.

Theme boards for Elizabethan design.

Skopos think that their success results from a variety of reasons, in particular product range, company flexibility and comprehensive service. Another reason is the high technical specification that the goods have to meet. Stringent standards are set to ensure that fabrics conform to high quality levels. Quality control takes place throughout production.

You have been asked to design a new fabric range for a major textile company. The theme is to be 'The natural world'. Create the theme board which will resource your designing. Try to include as many visual sources as possible, together with explanatory notes. Then take images from the board to develop designs for the fabrics.

Fabrics can be treated for flame retardance (to meet legislative demands) and soil resistance. These processes are applied during the manufacturing process, and conform with British Standard specifications.

RESISTANT

FLAME RETARDANT · SOIL RESISTANT
fRSr

skopos
FABRICS & WALLCOVERINGS

The fabrics are also subject to testing in the Skopos laboratory. These tests are to ensure that the quality and durability of the textiles are maintained. Tensile strength is tested by checking stretch on both warp and weft of the fabric. Yarn is tested to see the amount of abrasion it will take before breaking. Woven fabric is tested to see the degree of surface abrasion possible before **pilling** occurs. The durability of colour is tested by wet and dry rubbing tests.

Martindale abrasion machine and material being tested.

Carry out your own abrasion tests by stretching two pieces of the same fabric onto a board. One should be wet, the other left dry. Rub the edge of a coin or a piece of sandpaper on a block over the two pieces repeatedly. Note whether the wet or dry fabric shows signs of wear first and whether the colour is lost before the fabric itself begins to wear.

Skopos flame retardant/soil resistant logo.

Kite mark.

Fabrics for furnishings would usually be expected not to stretch a great deal or, if they do stretch, they should recover and show very little increase in length. You can test this by setting up a frame from which you can suspend a fabric sample. You must make sure that the weight is attached safely and cannot fall on your feet.

Diagram of apparatus.

- Mark two reference points with a pen and measure the length (*L1*).
- Add the 3 kg weight for 10 seconds, then measure the final length (*L2*).
- Remove the weight and measure the fabric flat (*L3*).
- Work out the percentage stretch by using $\frac{L2-L1}{L1} \times 100$.
- Work out the percentage stretch after removal of weight (residual extension) by $\frac{L3-L1}{L1} \times 100$.

A low residual extension means the fabric has good **elasticity**.

Some fabrics absorb water and other liquids easily. It can be the weave and/or the fibre which determine the absorbency.

- First, weigh your fabric sample in a container you already know the weight of and calculate the original (dry) mass of the sample.
- Immerse the fabric for 20 minutes in tap water (weight it down, otherwise it is likely to float).
- Remove excess water by shaking the fabric 10 times at 1 second intervals.
- To find out how much water has been absorbed, weigh the fabric sample again and, by subtracting the dry mass from the wet mass, calculate the mass of water absorbed.

The results are normally shown as a percentage, using

$$\frac{\text{mass of water absorbed by the sample}}{\text{original dry mass of the sample}} \times 100$$

Part of the Skopos philosophy is the principle of Designer/Manufacturer. As part of their service Skopos design the product and also manufacture it. The undoubted success of this for Skopos is due in no small part to their creativity and

technical expertise. It is also due to the reliability and consistency of their products which have earned for themselves a niche in the quality market.

It is possible to test waterproofness by seeing how resistant a fabric is to water spray. Use a watering can or spray nozzle to direct 250 ml water at a sample of fabric stretched over an embroidery hoop and held horizontally. When the spray has stopped, the sample should be turned upside down and tapped firmly, twice, to remove excess water. The amount of spray absorbed can best be described using these diagrams to judge the rate of absorbency.

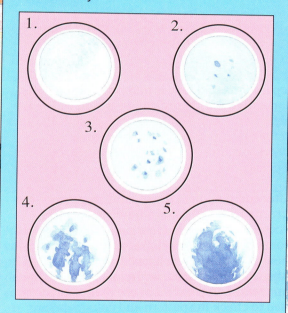

You should now understand:
- **about good working practices,**
- **materials and the finishes used,**
- **quality control,**
- **marketing,**
- **testing fabrics,**
- **designing.**

You will now be able to complete the task below which may form part or all of your coursework.

As a member of the design team for a well-known manufacturer of interior furnishing ranges you have been asked to design an additional scheme for their shops. The range is for decorating one of the following:

- a young child's playroom,
- a teenager's bedroom,
- the dormitory in an outdoor activity centre.

You will need to follow through the full design process, not forgetting to research your market and your target audience.
With labelled drawings giving details of colour, fabric and materials, display your designs.
Select one of the items from your range and make it up to meet your own design specifications.

You could compare different types of fabric for all these tests. It might be useful to work with the science department to conduct the tests.

What conclusions can be drawn from the results of your testing?

Finishing

Many fabrics for use as soft furnishing are required by law to be made flame retardant. This finish is applied in very precisely measured quantities within a foam. The fabric is then dried on the stenter and baked. It may then receive a final neutral wash and have a fixer applied to fix the dye or it may be treated further with a chemical to make the fabric resistant to staining. Stain resistance is important for fabrics which are to be used in public buildings like schools, hospitals and theatres to help prevent them from looking dirty quickly and to reduce cleaning bills.

At the end of the printing and application of any special finishes the fabric will be stentered, dried and baked before the final inspection.

Loom state

Bake

Wash

F.R.

Stenter
Dry Bake

Inspect

Desize → Wash → Slinge Bleach

Print ← Stenter Weave Straighten ← Wash

F.R. → Stenter Dry → Bake

Stenter Dry ← Solufix On Autofoam ← Neutral Wash

You will now be able to complete the task below which may form part or all of your coursework.

Experiment with printing, such as block, screen or stencil, using simple designs which could be used for household items and soft furnishing.

Use one or more of your experiments to make into items which could be used in a situation or place you have identified. Look at the range of special finishes which could be used for your products. Identify which would be essential/useful for your product and say why this is so.

You should now understand:
- **industrial applications of printing,**
- **quality control and assurance,**
- **the application of special finishes to fabrics.**

The history of Aquascutum

In Victorian times men and women did not buy their clothes 'ready made' or '**off the peg**' as we do today. If you wanted or needed a new suit or dress, you went to a tailor if you were a man, or a dressmaker if you were a woman, to be measured and choose a style to be made up especially for you. Later on dressmakers began to design their own collections of clothes for the spring and autumn and display them to their clients at shows. We are now familiar with these twice yearly extravaganzas, in particular those held in London and Paris.

Only wealthy people could afford to have their clothes made for them. Poorer people, especially men, often bought second-hand clothes or had them provided by their employer if they were servants. Many women who were poor made their own clothes or did dressmaking to earn money.

> Find out about the type of clothes people were wearing in the 1800s. Include all classes of society, and men, women and children. Produce an illustrated report.

In 1851 Prince Albert was busy helping to organise the Great Exhibition, which was to be a shop window for the whole of Europe to come and see what we could manufacture here in Britain. At that time there was a small high class tailor's shop in Regent Street, London who made high quality suits for men. At this shop they were trying to find a way of shower-proofing the wool cloth used to make their overcoats. The sheep's fleece is naturally rainproof as it contains lanolin which causes the water to run off the fleece without being absorbed. When wool is processed these natural oils are removed, leaving the yarn or fabric into which it is made very absorbent. This can be a useful property: a woollen garment can absorb up to 40% of its own weight in water before it feels wet. This makes wool a good fibre for wearing next to the skin if you need to be kept warm but not feel damp and clammy if you perspire.

> Think of circumstances when woollen garments might be used for these properties. Make a list and share it with the rest of your working group. Now think about the properties of other fibres and consider whether these could be used in the same way. Write up your conclusions.

By 1853, the company had succeeded in making a soft, flexible fabric which repelled the rain. They called it 'Aquascutum', a name derived from Latin meaning 'watershield'. The difficult pronunciation of the name ensured that it attracted a lot of attention at the Great Exhibition and orders flooded in from all over Europe. The coats soon became a status symbol, as well as being a high fashion, but practical, garment. Men wore them even when the weather was fine!

What we wear to protect us from the rain today bears little resemblance to the heavy overcoats worn from the nineteenth century up until the 1950s. The original coats made by Aquascutum were made to last and were also worn by soldiers in the Crimean war to keep them warm and dry. A cutter at Aquascutum also designed and cut a coat with a loose sleeve to give Lord

Edward, Prince of Wales, wearing an Aquascutum coat.

Raglan freedom of movement when he was leading the Charge of the Light Brigade. This became known as the raglan sleeve.

The son of Queen Victoria, Edward, Prince of Wales, loved clothes and, having seen friends wearing the Aquascutum coat, asked his tailor to make one using the same cloth. The tailor tried to buy some from the company but they refused to sell, so Prince Edward became an Aquascutum customer. Other royal family members became clients in later years.

In the late 1890s Aquascutum moved to 100 Regent Street, where it still has its headquarters today.

In 1914, at the start of the First World War, the misery of trench warfare was made worse by the lack of waterproof protection given by the poor quality cotton coats supplied to the officers. The coats were also unlined and so did not provide any warmth in the cold winter months. Aquascutum

offered to provide waterproof coats which they promised to replace free of charge if they let in water. There was little risk of this because the company tested their coats with fire hoses! These coats became known as trenchcoats and

> Research the range of rainwear garments available for men, women or children in your local shops. Compile a database to record information about the styles, fibres, fabrics and any special waterproofing methods used. Make recommendations about which are the best buys for, for example, someone who wants a showerproof garment that packs easily for a Duke of Edinburgh expedition, or a warm, waterproof, winter coat. You could also test a selection of waterproof or showerproof garments owned by students in your group.

this style is still used for rainwear today. During the 1914–8 War Aquascutum developed their range of clothes for women. They adapted the coat that they had developed for the soldiers and this quickly became a popular style for men and women (and remains so today). Aquascutum clothes have always been expensive, although the prices in 1910 seem very low when judged by today's standards. Then a standard coat cost £3.15, one lined with fur £12.60 and a smart evening cloak £4.20!

A trenchcoat.

Aquascutum suit for a woman.

When war came again in 1939, Aquascutum provided coats to the Allied Forces and made coats for sailors on winter convoys and jackets for airmen on night bombing raids. After the end of the war the export market began to boom and the range became particularly popular in the USA. In 1948 Aquascutum opened a showroom in New York, and a factory in Canada now supplies the whole American continent. In 1953 Sir Edmund Hillary and Sherpa Tensing Norkey conquered Everest wearing hooded jackets and trousers made from a material

called 'Wyncol D.711', made from cotton and nylon and now used for making Aquascutum raincoats. This fabric was tested in a wind tunnel and withstood a wind force of 100 mph.

Aquascutum continues to develop styles and ranges to keep in the forefront of the fashion industry in Britain. They make high quality clothes for men and women in a traditional style, which is very popular in other countries and has ensured the company's continued prosperity. In 1990 70% of their turnover was from export sales and the company was awarded its fifth Queen's Award for Export Achievement. At the same time as being leaders in fashion, they also continue to develop new fabrics, as they did in the 1850s, so that the traditional styles are updated and improved to make full use of modern technology.

They now use microfibre fabrics, produced exclusively for them, to make raincoats in styles developed from their original trenchcoat. Microfibre is a polyester fibre which has been modified to make it 'breathable'. It can be made into a variety of fabrics which are light and resilient and can be treated to make them showerproof.

The company are also producing collections of clothes for men and women in the spring and autumn of each year. These clothes are made using high quality, mostly natural fabrics, some of which are treated to make them waterproof. For example, linen has been treated with resin to make a mac with a 'crumpled' look which was very fashionable in 1995.

Aquascutum clothes are very popular in Japan, so in 1994 they had a major expansion there, by opening 130 shops-within-shops. An Aquascutum outlet is also planned in China.

In 1995 the factory in Kettering built a laboratory so that fabrics could be tested on the site. This provides a valuable service to the designers, cutters and machinists and helps with the continued development of fabrics and production techniques.

The resin-treated linen mac.

Microfibre fabric.

You should now understand:
- **how to recognise the need for a particular design,**
- **IT applications,**
- **quality control and assurance.**

You will now be able to complete the task below which may form part of your coursework.

Examine the styles which are traditional to British clothes and show examples for men and women.

Look at the traditional styles of other countries or cultures and identify why these have developed in this way. Reasons may include heritage, religion, climate, available resources and technology.

Manufacture at Aquascutum

Aquascutum identifies its core values as 'making high performance clothes' and 'creating exciting fashion in British design'. Neither of these can be fulfilled without the closest attention to detail at all stages.

A design team based in London takes full responsibility for originating all Aquascutum designs. Part of their brief is to retain, in their designs, those elements for which Aquascutum has a reputation, that is craftsmanship and high quality fabrics. They have also to make best use of new high technology fabrics. These are fabrics which have been developed using the most up-to-date knowledge in fibre and fabric manufacture, such as microfibre. In effect the designers have to combine the best of the old with the best of the new.

Once the designs for new garments have been approved a sample is made up. This could be done either in the London design headquarters or the Kettering manufacturing base.

Aquascutum logo.

In making up the garment the sample workers are not only making the design drawings into a reality, they are also working out the specifications for the cutters and machinists in the factory. The **specification** includes all the detailed information needed to make the garment and would include such things as seam allowances, buttonhole placements and top stitching detail.

In the Aquascutum manufacturing process, quality is of the utmost importance. The fabrics used and the production processes are of a very high standard. Consequently the clothing sells for a high price. However, despite the importance placed on 'quality' there is no room for waste, neither waste of fabric nor waste of time. The aim, when placing the pattern pieces on the fabric, is to find the arrangement which gives the least wastage of fabric, known as the **lay**. It is important, however, to ensure that the grain lines for each piece are correct and all fabric designs that should match do so.

Company crest.

Design a raincoat which is to appeal to young teens. The garment should be suitable for protection against the weather and to suit the lifestyle and fashion needs of young people. Suggest fabrics, colours, detailing, and draw your design with back and front views. If possible, gather comments about your design from people in your target customer group. Adjust your design where needed to take into account any comments or criticisms.

To make sure that grain lines are correctly placed:
- Place the grain line so that it looks parallel to the selvedge. (Selvedge is formed by weft threads going round the first and last warp threads on the loom.)
- Pin one end of the grain line and measure (at right angles) the distance to the selvedge.
- Measure from the other end of the grain line to the selvedge and adjust the pattern piece until the two measurements are exactly the same. Pin this end, then pin the remainder of the pattern piece into place.

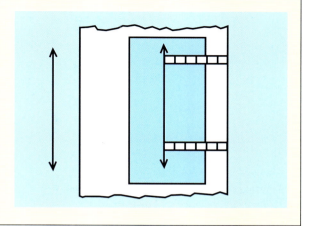

A grain line on a pattern piece (often referred to as the straight grain) should run parallel to the warp threads.

When making clothes as Aquascutum do, or indeed as anyone does using these methods, the end-result is a 3-dimensional object (the garment) made from 2-dimensional materials (the fabric).

Working as a group disassemble an unwanted garment by either unpicking all the seams or cutting, very carefully, along the seams. Keep careful note of which pattern pieces constituted which part of the garment. Iron the fabric pieces flat.

From what you have discovered in this exercise can you identify some of the pattern pieces shown here?

Even if the pieces are not exactly like yours try to work out what the variations might be.

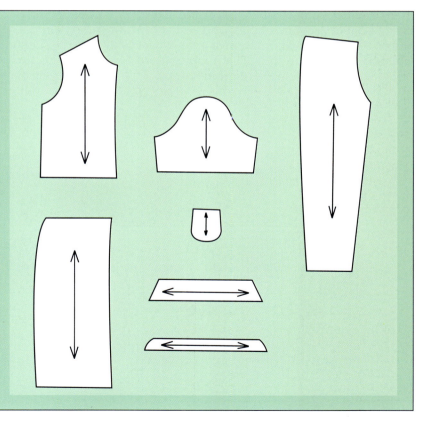

Draw the pattern piece for a long sleeve and mark on it:

- the wrist edge,
- the top of the sleeve at the shoulder (sleeve head),
- the underarm seam.

Compare pattern pieces for different kinds of sleeve, such as magyar, bishop and raglan. Look at how differences in the 2-dimensional pattern pieces produce the different 3-dimensional shapes of the finished sleeves. You could also look at the relationship between other 2-dimensional pattern pieces and their 3-dimensional made-up parts, such as skirts, trouser legs, collars, etc.

It would be possible to swathe fabric round the human form to cover the body and look attractive (traditional dress from which country does just that?). Different techniques must be used to achieve other results. The fabric pieces must be cut to accommodate the body shape, and also make allowance for the curves, angles and movement of the body. This is why pattern pieces look very odd to the uninformed eye.

Clothing manufacturers need to produce large quantities of their garments. This must be done in the most cost effective way, by, for example, economising on time wherever possible. One way of speeding up the cutting out process is to cut out more than one garment at a time. This is done by placing layers of fabric on top of each other and cutting them all together.

Traditionally the cutter used pattern blocks which were positioned correctly and then chalked round, using special tailor's chalk. Large shears or an electric knife were used to cut out the pieces. Experienced cutters, using the band knife, can cut many thicknesses manually.

At Aquascutum they use up-to-date technology which not only further speeds the process but is also highly accurate. The **lay** is worked out using a computer program. This program is linked to the Gerber cutter which, following the computer's instructions, cuts the fabric with a rotary knife. The layers of fabric are held in place by suction from underneath the cutting bed. Using this process 20 layers of woollen, or 50 layers of cotton, fabric can be cut at one time.

Cross section of the Gerber.

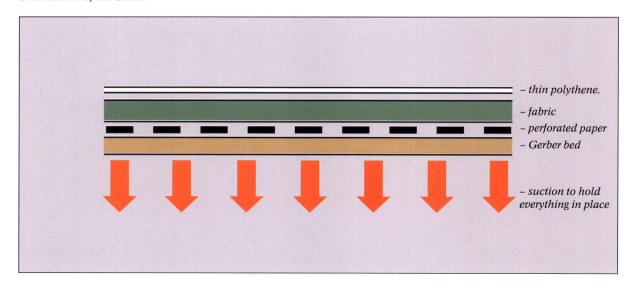

– *thin polythene.*
– *fabric*
– *perforated paper*
– *Gerber bed*

– *suction to hold everything in place*

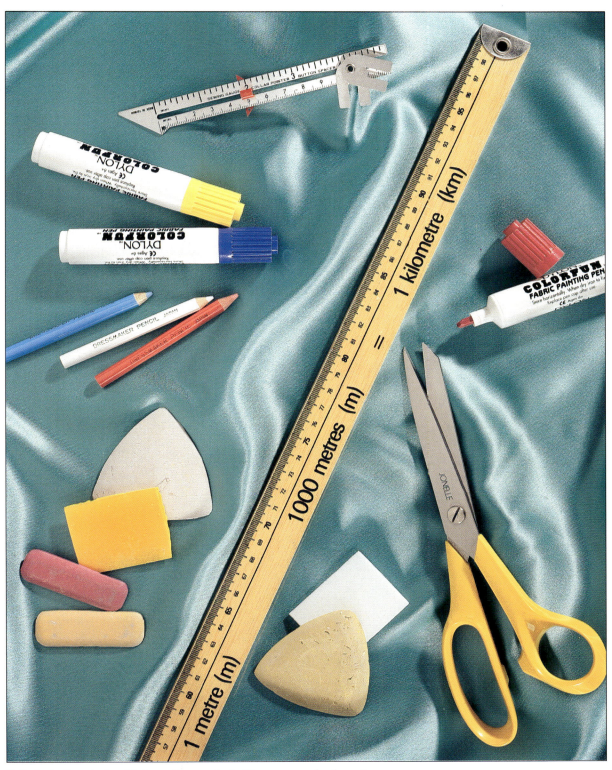

*Tailor's chalk and other fabric marking products. These are now for domestic use,
but they are a spin off from trade/ manufacturing.*

The Gerber is only used for plain fabrics which do not have to match across seams. At Aquascutum even the smallest of checks (3 mm) are made to match.

Where there are joins on the garment, for example at the shoulder and side seams, it is vital that the checks and stripes on the fabric match. Although this makes no difference to the **wear** of the garment, it looks much better. This is the responsibility of the machinist, but the task is made possible by the skills of the cutter:
* first, the layers of the check fabric must be positioned so that the identical parts of a check are directly on top of each other,
* secondly, the pattern pieces which are to match must be laid correctly on the fabric.

There could be as many as 38 layers of a medium-weight wool. The matching is held by 'pins', which are 120 mm long spikes as thick as darning needles.

Whilst cutting, the cutter needs to hold the fabric in place with the other hand which is covered by a chain mail glove to protect it.

The smallest Aquascutum check (life size).

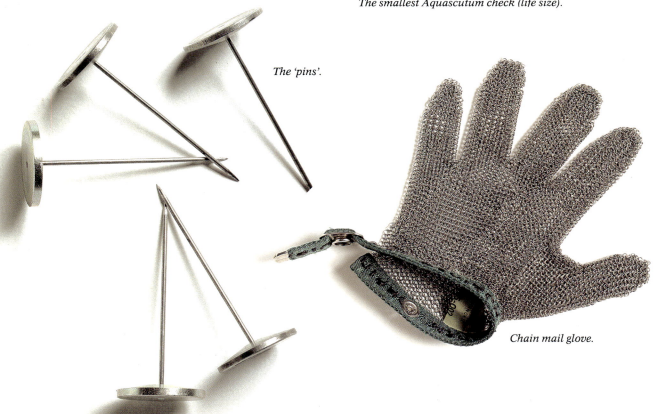

The 'pins'.

Chain mail glove.

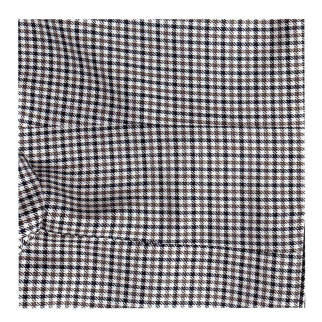

Seam with well-matched checks.

Ill-matched seam.

Look in clothing shops at garments which have a check or stripe fabric. Do the stripes/checks match at the shoulder/side seam? If they do, is it true for all the garments in that range or have you picked up a good one? Note the price of the garments. Compare prices of similar garments. Can you draw any conclusions about well- matched fabrics and price of garment?

Once the garment has been cut out the stiffenings are attached. These give the garment more body and make it hang well (underlinings). They are also used to give extra firmness for areas of fastenings (down the front for buttons and buttonholes) or for areas like collars (interlinings). These should not be confused with the lining which is the, usually, lightweight shell put inside a garment so that it does not cling to the body where it should not and moves more freely. Thicker linings are used where warmth is required in a garment.

Many of the interlinings used are fusible, that is they can be made to adhere to the fabric of the outer garment. Having been cut out in quantity (as previously described), separate bundles of the garment piece and its matching interlining are passed to the fusing machine. Here a worker matches the interlining to, for example, the collar. The two pieces travel on a short conveyer belt over the fusing bed (hidden from view), and emerge on a conveyer belt the other side to be collected and piled with other fused pieces by another worker. This particular element of the work is quite labour intensive.

Fusing machine.

After this stage is complete the different pieces of the garment are put into bundles ready for the machinists.

Industrial sewing machines perform a variety of tasks. The straight stitch machine does just what it says, as does the longseamer (used to attach front facings). Overlockers neaten and trim. There are machines for making buttonholes and for the **bartack** of buttonholes; there are machines for sewing on buttons. The shanker winds the thread round the 'stalk' of the thread attaching the button to make it stronger. The pocket slasher cuts and binds slit pockets in linings, and the aptly named plonker does temporary tacking stitches, by plonking into the fabric to make long stitches. The machines are very fast, very powerful and very sophisticated.

Industrial machines.

The machinists do not make a whole garment but each worker plays their part in the production process. It is not strictly a production line as they are working independently on their own bundles. The machinist completes all the work required on each bundle before the bundle goes on to the next stage of the process. This is an example of **batch production**.

In the manufacture of a raincoat the sections on which a machinist works are:
- piecing up (small parts, epaulettes, cuff tabs etc.),
- making up sleeves, collars, backs,
- attaching facings to fronts,
- pockets, linings and side seams,
- sleeve insertion,
- hems.

After the machinist has finished each of the process bundles they undergo a quality control check. If faults are found the piece is not discarded, but unpicked, recut or whatever is necessary so that the piece can be restitched correctly. This is because the fabrics used are extremely expensive; to waste even 50 cm of fabric costing £100+ per metre is a lot to lose. 'Bitting' takes place after each machining process. This is trimming of ends and general tidying up.

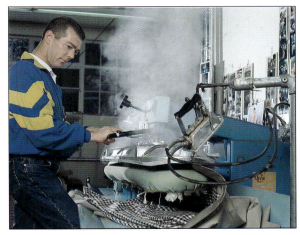

The Hoffman presser.

Pressing also takes place at each stage. Either an iron rather similar to a domestic iron or the Hoffman presser are used. The latter is a large machine with two hinged surfaces, rather like a large toasted sandwich maker. The fabric is positioned on the lower surface and the top surface lowered on to it. Pressing is achieved by the action of heat and steam.

The quality control continues throughout the manufacturing process. When the garment is complete, apart from joining lining to garment at the hem, the final check takes place. If any faults are found at this stage mistakes can still be rectified because the workers can still get to the inside of the garment.

Once the hems are complete the garment goes to 'audit'. This is the very last stage: final pressing, mark removal wherever necessary, and the final quality assessment. In audit the garments are prepared for delivery to shops and protected by a polythene cover.

To secure the orders Aquascutum sales personnel visit the retail outlets. They carry drawings of the designs and cloth sample books, detailing which styles are available in which fabrics. The shop buyers make their choice, the goods are delivered, and the customer makes the purchase.

You should now understand:
- **how to design for a particular market, taking into account current fashion trends,**
- **IT applications,**
- **industrial processes for making clothes,**
- **the use of systems and control in manufacture,**
- **quality control and quality assurance.**

You will now be able to complete the task below which may form part or all of your coursework.

Make up a garment for yourself or a child. You may use or modify a commercial pattern, but treat the exercise as though you were the sample worker for a major manufacturer.
- Construct the garment.
- Provide a specification sheet for bulk production (make a note of seam allowances used, numbers of buttons, pocket details, hem depths, order of construction, amount of fabric used, etc.).
- Keep a careful record of the amount of time you spend on the garment.
- Using your IT skills, generate a cost sheet for the garment. List all the materials used and cost your time at the amount you or your friends are paid for Saturday/holiday jobs.

Socks for everyone

Socks are an item of clothing worn by people of all ages and many nationalities.

We wear socks for a variety of reasons, the same sorts of reasons that help us to make decisions about our other clothes, for example they suit the weather and they go with the rest of the outfit.

The basic shape of the sock has not changed – it must fit a foot! However, you will discover that this basic shape has been developed in many ways so that there is now a wide product range available.

The start of the brainstorm.

Fashionable

I like the colour

My Socks

Practical

Working in a group or pairs brainstorm the different *reasons* people might have for their *choice* of sock. It might help if you think of different jobs, lifestyles and occasions to help you identify the socks that people might wear.
Compare and discuss your list with others in the class.

 *Background*

It is quite likely that all the socks worn by people around you were bought ready made; but this was not always the case. Before commercial manufacturing processes were developed socks were made in the home. Even after socks became readily available in the shops many people wore hand-knitted socks. Hand knitting is a slower process than using a knitting machine, so it takes much longer to make a pair of socks by hand.

Can you draw any conclusions about the different lifestyle of those people (usually women) who used to knit socks? What are your conclusions?

There is one age group who, even today, frequently wear hand-knitted footwear – babies. Can you decide why this is so ?

A 1940s hand-knitted sock.

Production

The vast majority of socks worn today are produced commercially in factories.

In both the commercial and domestic manufacturing process socks are usually made as a tube, closed at one end. Sometimes the sock has a shaped toe and heel.

To be comfortable to wear, socks need to fit well but allow for ease of movement as the foot and ankle move. Well-fitting socks are as important as well-fitting shoes for developing feet. It is not only the shape in which a sock is made that gives a good fit; the way in which the fabric is constructed also makes a difference.

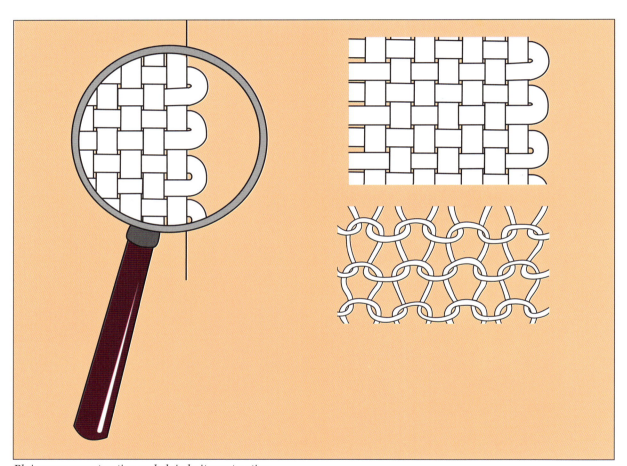

Plain weave construction and plain knit construction.

Test the stretch in pieces of knitted and woven fabric.

Stretch the fabric in all directions. Which would be the most suitable for making socks?

Why is the construction method you have chosen the most suitable?

Fibres for socks

When choosing socks it is very easy to see what they look like and whether or not they will go with your outfit. The fibre content is less obvious but just as important because fibres have different characteristics, called fibre qualities or properties. Some fibres are warm, others cool; some absorbent, others non-absorbent. Fibres can have more than one 'quality'. To find this out you need to read the label on the socks. The table below shows information about the qualities of different fibres from which socks could be made.

For each fibre in the table write a sentence explaining why that particular fibre might be chosen to be made into a pair of socks. Investigate the origin of the fibres (from what and how they are made) and the structure of the fibres (what the fibre looks like when it is magnified) and how this contributes to the qualities.

	strong	cool	warm	easily washed	elastic	absorbent
cotton	●	●		●		●
wool			●			●
nylon	●			●		
silk		●	●			●
lycra	●			●	●	
acrylic	●			●		
polyester	●			●		

Think of what people want from a sock when they wear it, for example sports socks have to be very absorbent. Sometimes fibres are combined in the manufacturing process. Include any combinations you think might be a good idea or have seen.

Carry out a survey to find out where people buy their socks. Find out as well if they had any particular reasons for choosing their particular socks. You could use a database to help you. Make a chart to show your findings.

Sock PURCHASE

Name	Place of Purchase	Reason for choice
Alice	M+S (chain store)	Liked colour
Shamir	Sports shop	Sport sock
Edward	Market stall	fashionable
Rupert	A present	didn't choose them
Blondell	Supermarket chain store	Mum said were cheap enough
Chimi	Specialised sock shop	different from usual ones

Marketing

Now that you have discovered where people buy their socks, you can begin to look at comparative prices and availability.

Research the outlets where socks are sold. Group the different outlets according to the type of shop they are. Can you draw any conclusions about the target market from the prices, style of display, selling unit or any other factors about the socks?

Write a report or design a chart to summarise your findings.

You should now understand:
- **how to recognise the need for a design,**
- **how to plan and carry out research,**
- **the application of IT in research,**
- **materials and their applications,**
- **products and their applications.**

You will now be able to complete the task below which may form part or all of your coursework.

You have analysed the market range of socks. Now is the time to make your individual contribution. You are the design stylist and fibre expert. Design a sock for 'an occasion'. It can be a sports activity, a uniform, child's leisure wear – the choice is yours. The decoration on the sock can be either knitted in during the manufacturing process or applied as surface decoration after knitting.

- Draw the sock, say who or for what circumstance the sock is designed, and give explanatory notes of the design where necessary. Don't forget to say which fibre you have chosen and why.
- Construct a prototype.

By looking at the labels on socks in shops, or checking the descriptors in a catalogue, find the most common fibres from which socks are produced. What other information is given on the label?

Peta Flint Designs

Peta Flint designs and makes socks. But they are quite unlike most of the socks that you have researched so far. From a young age Peta was always fascinated by machinery, the way things were made and how they worked. She had a passion for motorbikes and devoted her energies to mending and rebuilding them. Her practical talents and skills were much wider than the mechanical world and she was also very interested in textiles.

She studied Textiles at Goldsmiths' College in London and it was whilst she was in London that she came across an ancient sock knitting machine, her first. The challenge then was to work out exactly what it did – and how it did it – equipment that was made in the 1800s tends not to have the instruction manual with it!

Peta Flint's workroom. The sock knitting machine is in the centre.

Imagine that you have no experience of machinery of any sort. Working in a small group, make *three* lists:
- equipment/machinery whose task and how it works is very obvious,
- equipment/machinery whose task and how it works is not easy to understand simply by looking at it,
- equipment/machinery whose task and how it works you'd like to understand.

The sock knitting machine has a circle of **latches** to make the loops. This results in the knitting coming out in a tube as the knitting yarn goes round and round the latches in a spiral.

Knitting is the construction of a textile using a continuous thread. This thread is formed into rows of loops, through which the thread passes, in loops, to make the next row of loops.

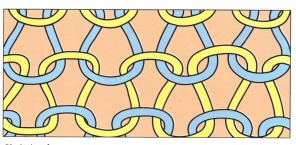

Knitting loops.

Flat bed knitting machines are also available (most domestic knitting machines are flat bed). Here the latches are in rows and the yarn, although travelling continuously, travels from left to right and then back right to left; giving flat pieces of knitting.

Hand knitting using two knitting pins gives the equivalent of a flat bed machine; hand knitting using four pins gives the equivalent of a sock knitting machine.

Nottingham was an area noted for stocking and sock manufacture, particularly during the nineteenth century. It was at Ruddington, a village near Nottingham, that Peta Flint set up the **Framework Knitters** Museum. Here she collected and restored all sorts of knitting machinery and learned about how they worked from some of the few surviving craftsmen still living in the area and working the old machinery. She even took apart and reconstructed a Victorian machine which had

2000 parts. She began to take particular interest in the sock knitting machine – this only has 80 parts!

Brainstorm the characteristics that you would say all pieces of machinery share. Think about, for example, a motor bike, a sewing machine and a food processor.

Whilst she was working at Ruddington, Peta's own collection of sock knitting machines grew. They had been produced right up until the 1940s and many were discovered in attics, having been forgotten for years. They are beautiful objects, shiny and black with brass fittings.

Sock knitting machine.

At the same time Peta Flint set up a group of knitters to produce socks for a specialist market. She has a simple **batch production** system.

There are hand knitters who knit the top of the sock, often in cable which is a way of knitting that looks like twisted rope or cable. There are also machine knitters who transfer the knitting produced by the hand knitters on to their machines and then complete the sock on the machine. This combination of hand and machine knitting was a new venture. All the knitters are trained by Peta herself, and she also designs and makes samples of the sock styles.

Cable stitch.

People work in their own homes and deliver their part of the sock to Peta who redistributes them to other workers and then fills the orders for shops and individuals. At all stages Peta acts as quality controller.

All of Peta Flint's workers are women, as were many of the workers in the nineteenth century. Some of the knitters in the nineteenth century also worked at home, but many more were based in the factories. Others worked in groups of eight or ten in the top rooms of specially constructed houses. These rooms ran the full length of the house and had windows on three sides to allow in the maximum light. It was traditionally the men who worked on the large machines whilst women worked the small ones. By the 1880s the smaller machines in the factories were linked together with one woman in charge of three machines. This can be seen as the beginning of the production line.

Manufacturers of the small knitting machines from the nineteenth century that Peta now uses developed additional targets for their sales. It was considered fashionable for the middle class woman to own a knitting machine and show her 'womanly' skills of creativity and gentility through knitting. Women who had a lower income also bought the machines, as a means of earning extra money for the family budget after the purchase price had been paid off by the first profits produced on the goods.

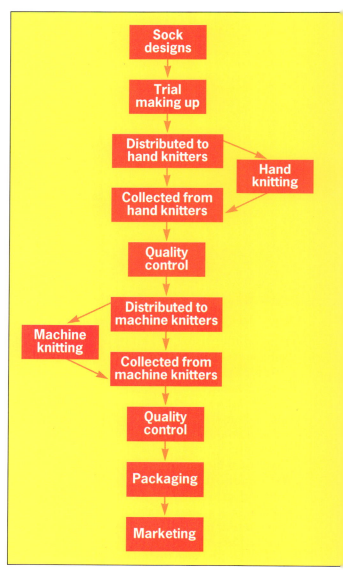

Peta Flint's production system.

The way in which Peta Flint organises her work can be seen as a **production line**, with different individuals taking responsibility for different manufacturing and production processes.
It is a production line with a difference in that, most of the time, the socks are knitted in the workers' own homes. **Outwork** is attractive to many people because they can fit their work around other things they need to do; it gives them a sort of flexibility. Much of the 'rag trade' (garment manufacture) is staffed by outworkers, who have sewing machines in their own homes and have bundles of part garments delivered to them to work on.

Trademark.

Many outworkers are women. Discuss with others in your group why you think this might be. Imagine yourself to be an outworker: what do you think the advantages and disadvantages might be for you?

It is not only the individual way of manufacture that makes the socks special. The fibres used are also of a very high quality – cashmere, fine cotton and wool. The fact that the production is labour intensive and the materials are such high quality, and therefore costly, means that the target market for the socks must be prepared to pay a higher than usual price for the socks. Peta Flint Socks are available from shops in Great Britain, and are also imported by boutiques in Italy and Austria.

peta flint ™

Peta Flint socks.

The success of the business was given a boost by a mail-order venture in a glossy magazine shortly before Christmas 1994. An article about Peta and her work was accompanied by a special offer to buy some of her socks at a bargain price. This resulted in far more orders than she had dreamed of, but her knitters worked very hard and all the orders were completed in time for Christmas.

The offer included a copy of the new mail-order catalogue. This has a sophisticated format which reflects the high quality of the goods that Peta and her team are producing. The photography aims to reflect the manufacturing process, for example a picture of the socks arranged around a knitting machine, and part of the target market, such as socks for hunting and fishing lain on a woodland floor. It also shows the Peta Flint trademark, her name.

machine which had become redundant as a result of increased automation and the demand for **mass production** that is cheaper and so the product can be priced lower. She has increased the range of choice in the market by providing high quality goods, and has trained a new generation of skilled workers. She has also provided employment for those workers, employment which is both unusual and creatively satisfying. The business has expanded considerably, but she intends to control the rate of growth to match the needs and demands of her family and lifestyle. She is also planning ahead to give herself time for designing so that the innovative aspects of her work are maintained.

Using both your IT skills and working by hand, design and plan the layout for an A4 folded sheet which is to be used as the catalogue for a sophisticated item of clothing. You may choose your own goods for the catalogue, but they must be for the expensive end of the market.

You will find it helpful to research which elements of advertising carry an implicit (or even explicit) message of 'quality'. You might also find it useful to look at the other end of the advertising market and analyse other, more brash, advertising tactics.

Think carefully about layout, language, colours, and the type of paper you would suggest using. Present the plan/layout for your catalogue to your group and describe for them the rationale behind your choices.

You should now understand:
- **how to recognise the need for a design,**
- **advertising and marketing,**
- **industrial applications,**
- **systems,**
- **quality control.**

You will now be able to complete the task below which may form part or all of your coursework.

Design and make a small textile item which would be for sale as a gift. Using your IT skills produce the page layout for the mail-order publicity material.
You will need to:
- identify and research your market,
- design the goods for sale,
- make the prototype,
- cost the goods.

Consider ways in which your manufacturing process could be streamlined to enhance efficiency.

Peta Flint has, through her sock-making enterprise, succeeded in many ways. She has fulfilled her own needs to be creative and practical, yet at the same time satisfying her passion for complicated machinery. She has revived and regenerated use of the sock knitting

Glossary

Applique
Work applied to or laid on another material.

Bartack
The stitches at the end of a buttonhole which prevent the fabric tearing beyond the buttonhole.

Batch production
A type of production in which a worker works on a number of identical elements which will eventually contribute to a whole product (garment). After quality control, the batch is then passed to another worker for the next stage of the construction process. For example, when the sleeves of 20 garments have been set in and checked, the batch of garments may then be passed to the next worker for hemming.

Contract basis
Goods produced for a particular client to a given specification.

Co-operative
A business owned and run jointly by its members with profits shared among them.

Database
A structured set of known facts stored in a computer.

Data Protection Act (1984)
Legal control over access to data stored in computers.

Design Consultancy
An individual or group who advise clients on interior decor.

Division of labour
The workforce carries out specialist tasks in the production process. Each worker carries out one part of the total assembly or manufacture. In mass production such a division of labour should lead to higher productivity.

Elasticity
The power to return to original size, springiness.

Flat bed knitting machine
A knitting machine which knits flat pieces of fabric.

Framework knitters
Workers who used early industrial knitting machines.

Franchise
Authorisation given to an individual or a group by a large company to sell its goods or services in a specified area.

Hide
The skin of an animal.

Industrial Revolution
A period of great change in Britain from about 1760 to 1830. Britain changed from being a predominantly agricultural nation with people living and working in villages, to an industrial nation with people mainly living and working in towns and cities.

Latches
Metal hooks which both carry and knit the yarn on a knitting machine.

Lay
The way pattern pieces are placed on fabric in the most economical fashion.

Marketing
The way goods are brought to sale. Marketing involves doing surveys, taking note of consumer needs and designing advertising campaigns.

Mass production
The production of large quantities by a standardised process.

Merchandise
Goods or articles for sale.

Module retailer
A retailer whose range of goods includes all or many of the articles needed for a particular purpose, for example, home decor.

Multiple
One of many shops belonging to the same firm, with branches in different places in the country. Often the term 'chain store' is used in place of multiple.

Off the peg
Clothes which are ready made.

Outwork
Work carried out in the home of the worker as opposed to in a factory or centralised setting.

Overheads
The general expenses of a business, the general running costs as distinct from business transactions.

Pantograph
An instrument which copies a plan or drawing on a different scale by a system of joined rods.

Pattern drop or design repeat
The element of a design which forms the section that is repeated down the length and across the width of a piece of fabric. It is sometimes called the pattern repeat.

Piece work
Work paid for by the amount produced.

Pilling
Small bobbles on the surface of fabric caused by friction.

Production line
A sequence of operations involved in the production of a commodity.

Prototype
A trial version or model made to help in the design of the final product.

Quality control
A system for maintaining standards in manufactured products by testing a sample of the output against the specification.

Retail
The selling of goods, usually in relatively small quantities, to members of the public.

Selvedge
The neat, firm edge formed by the weft thread turning round the first and last warp threads on a loom.

Specification
The features of a design which might include the materials to be used, their availability and cost; the sizes, uses and the intended market.

Warp
The threads placed first on the loom for the weaving process.

Wear
The way in which a garment shows (or does not show) deterioration during the time it is worn.

Weft
The thread which runs across the loom weaving in and out of the warp threads.

Wholesale
The selling of goods, usually in large quantities, to be retailed by others.

Index